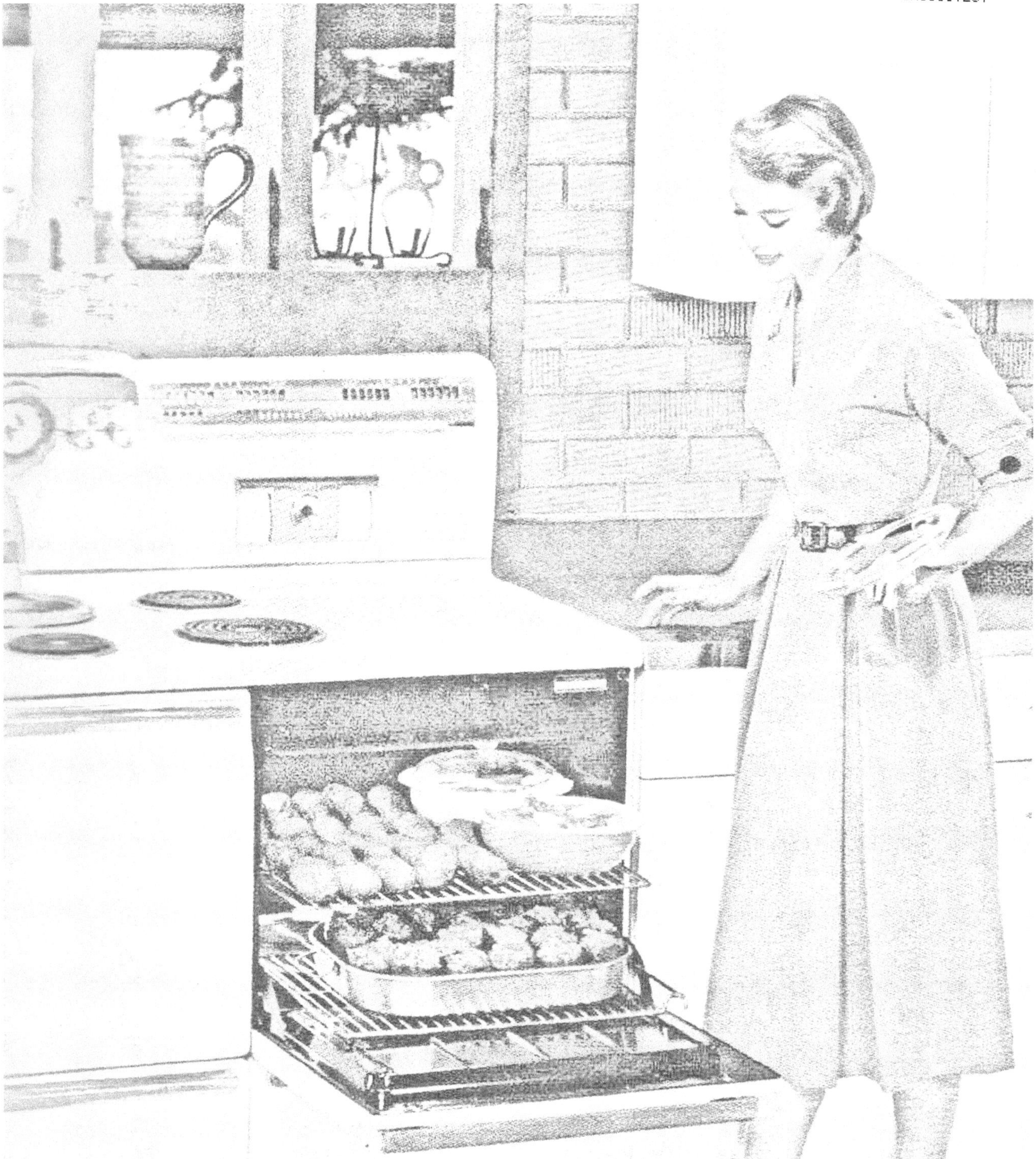

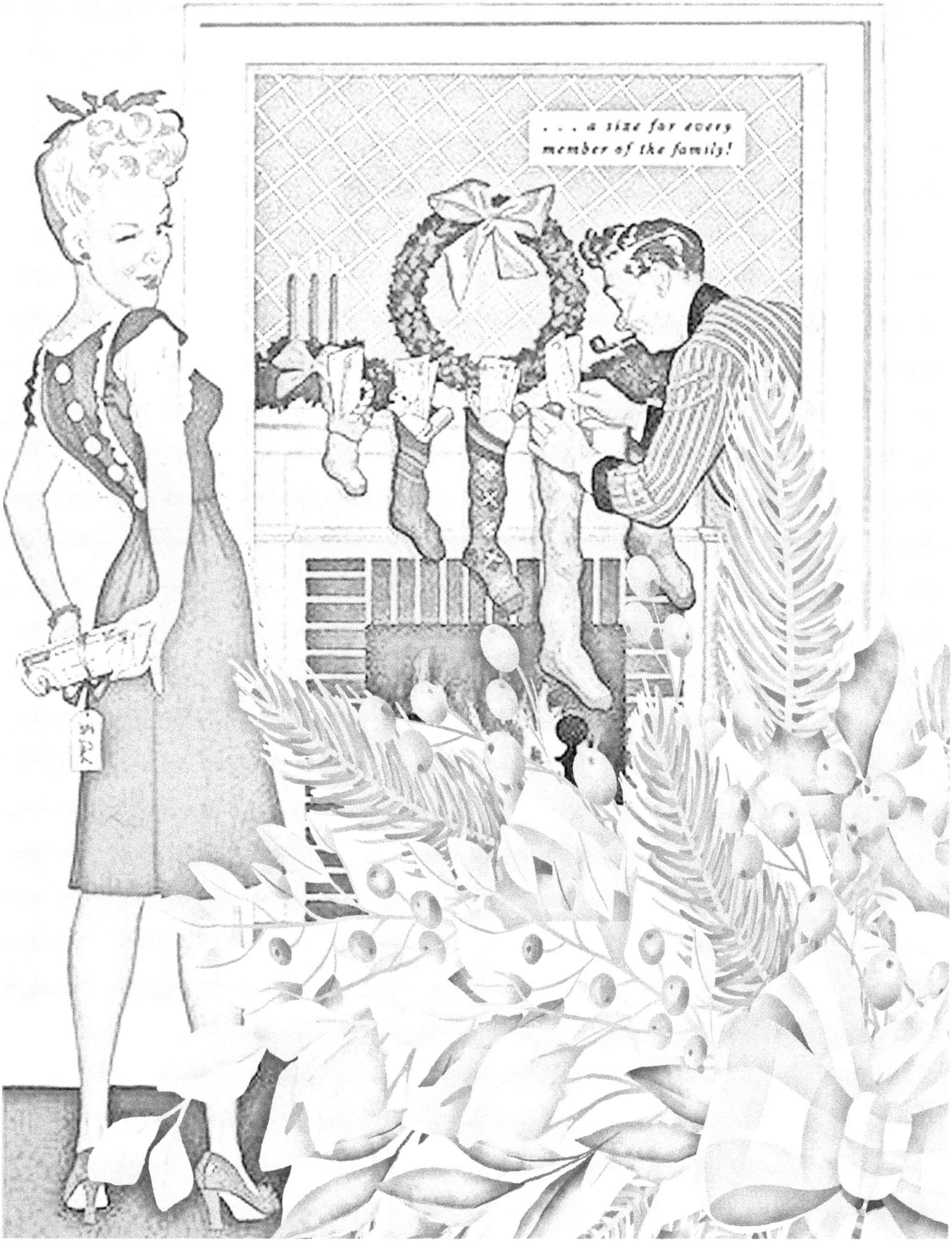
. . . a size for every
member of the family!

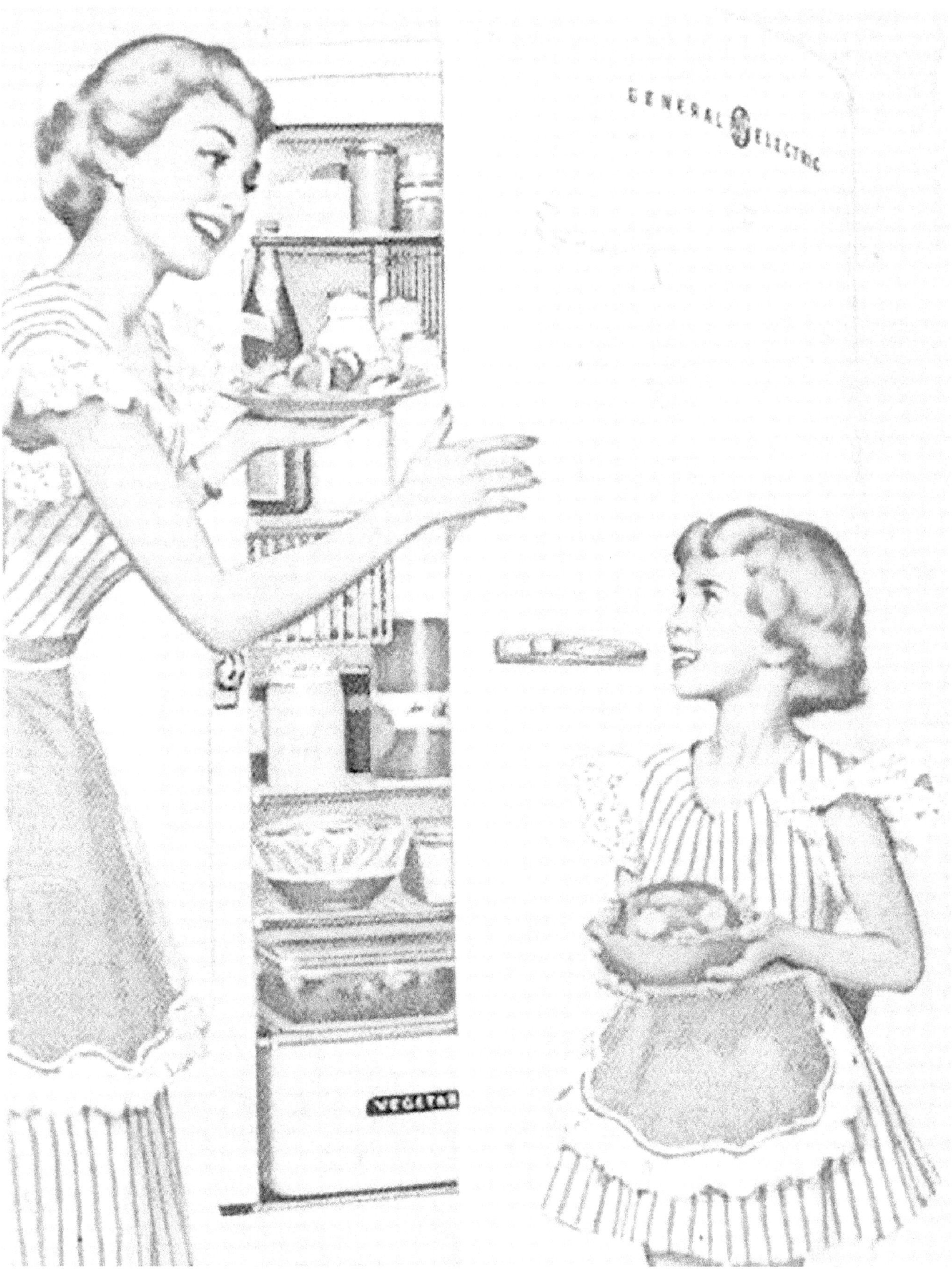
GENERAL ELECTRIC

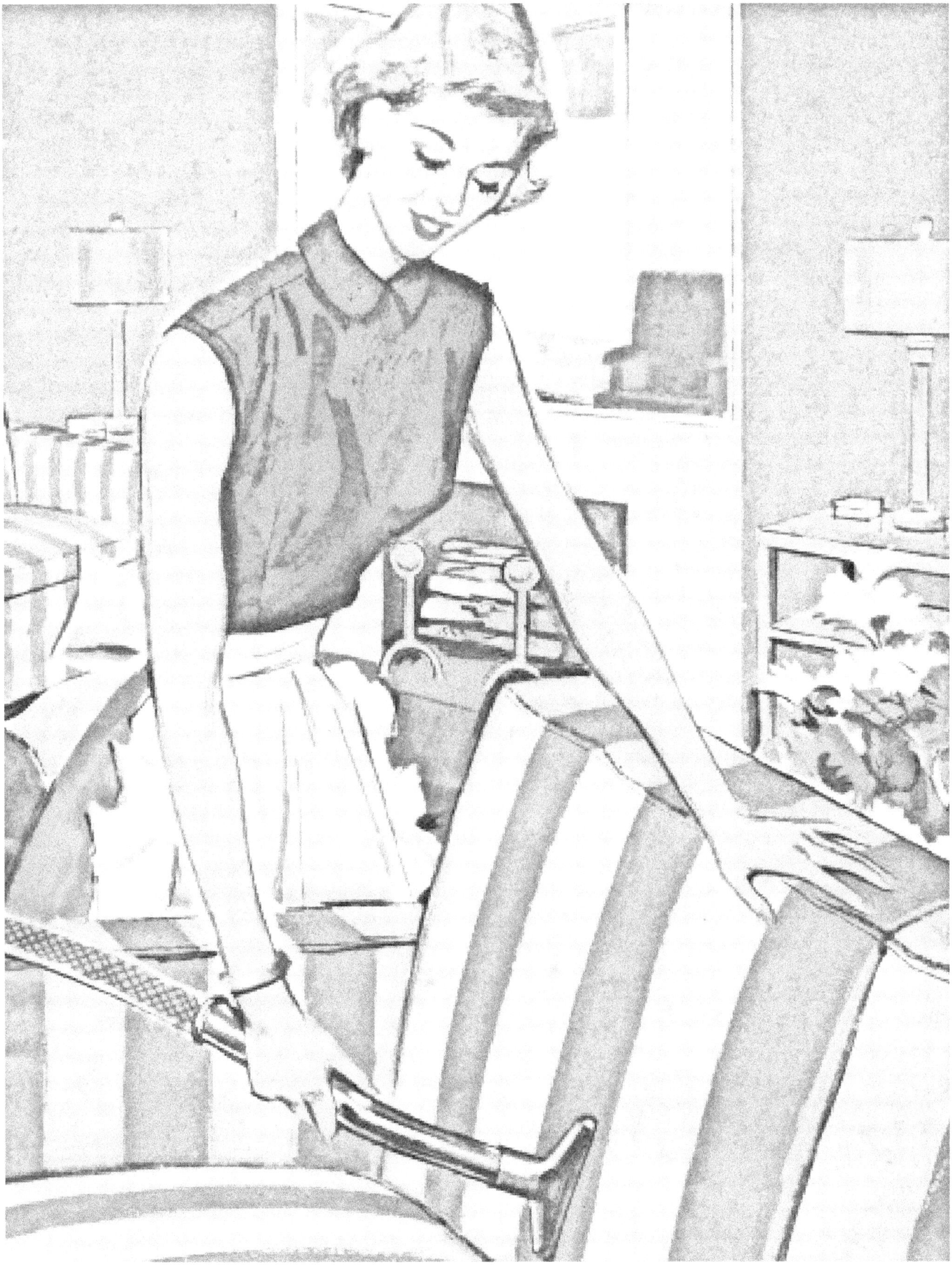

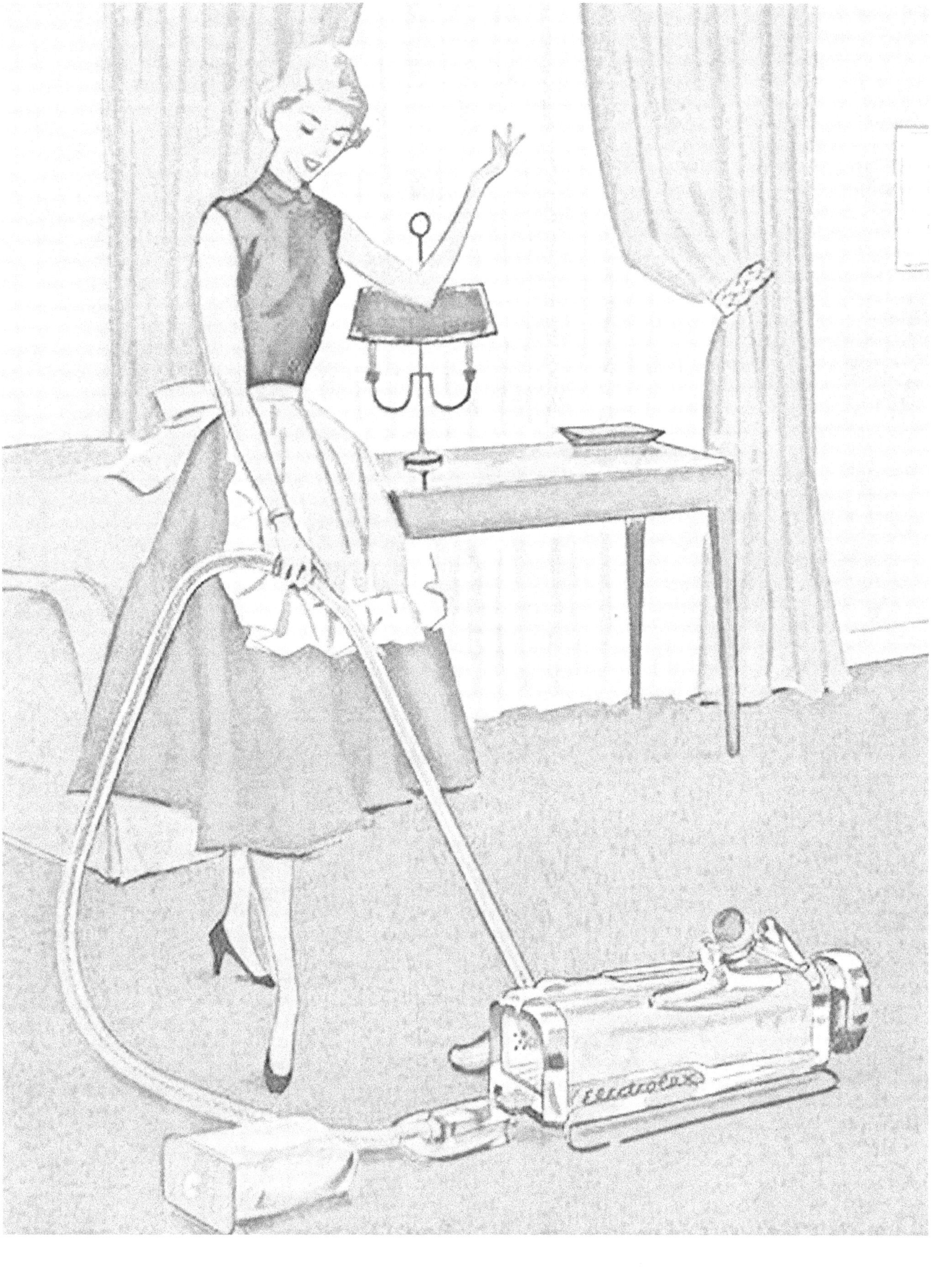
Electrolux

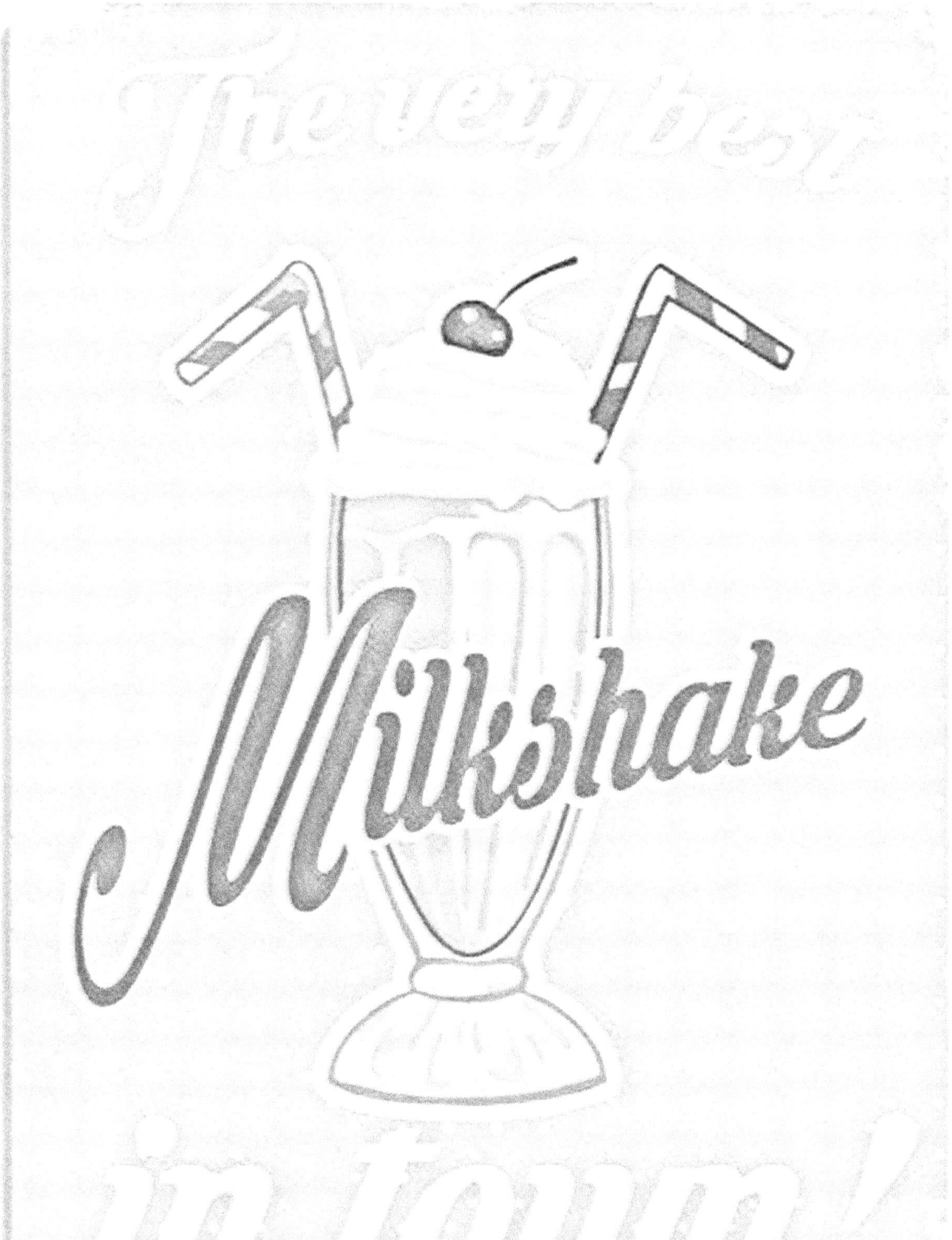
The very
Milkshake
in town!

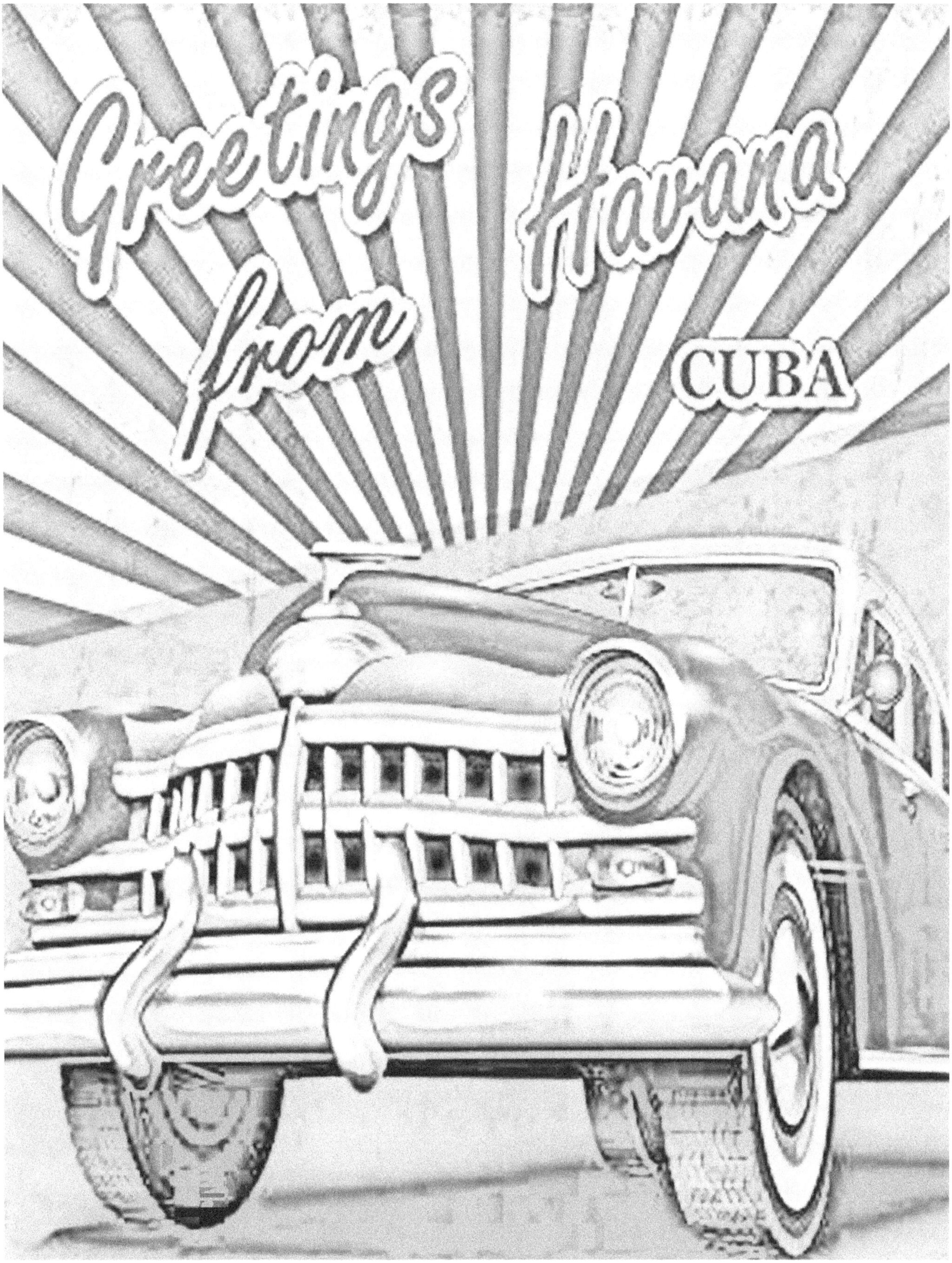
Greetings
from
Havana
CUBA

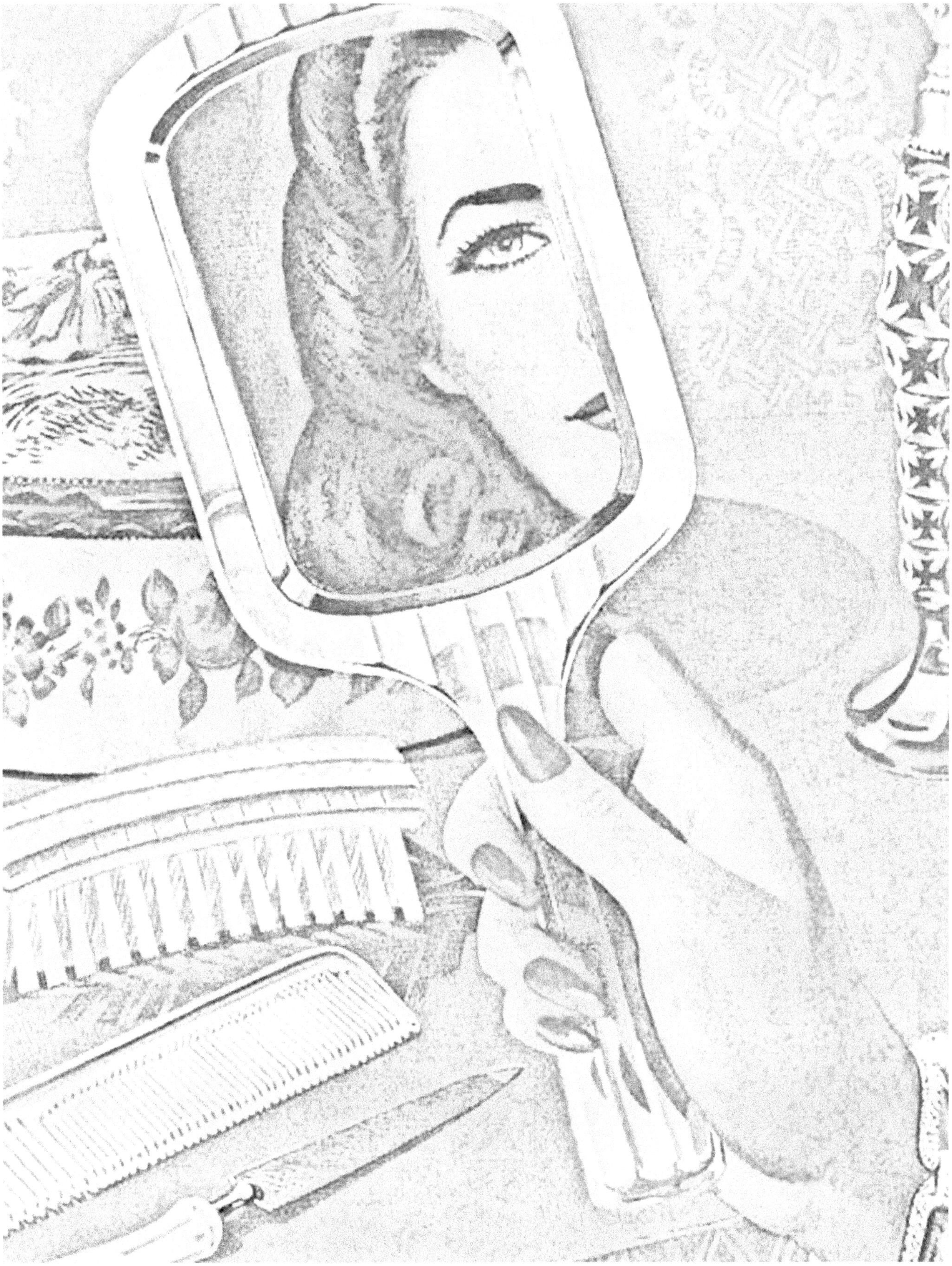

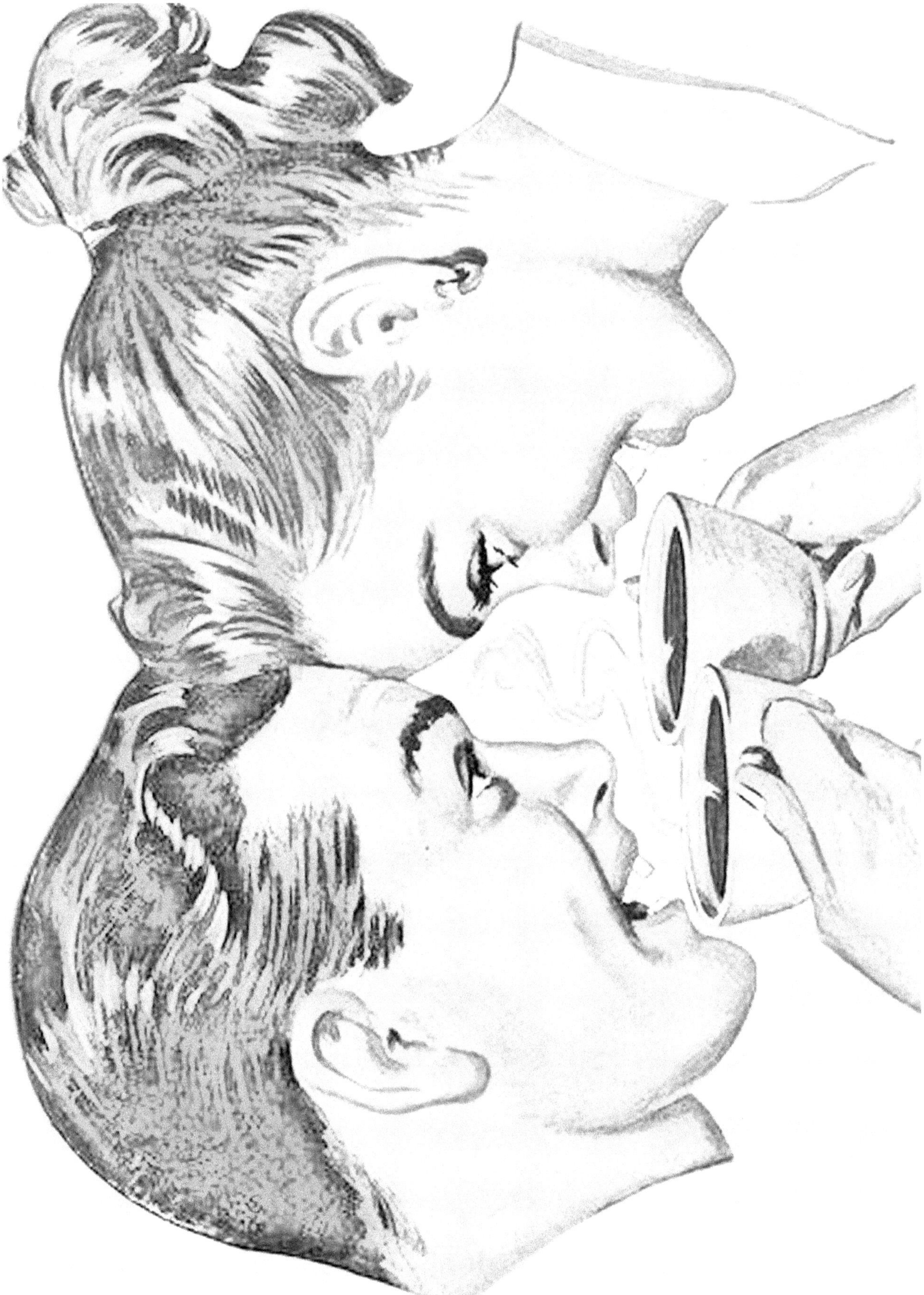

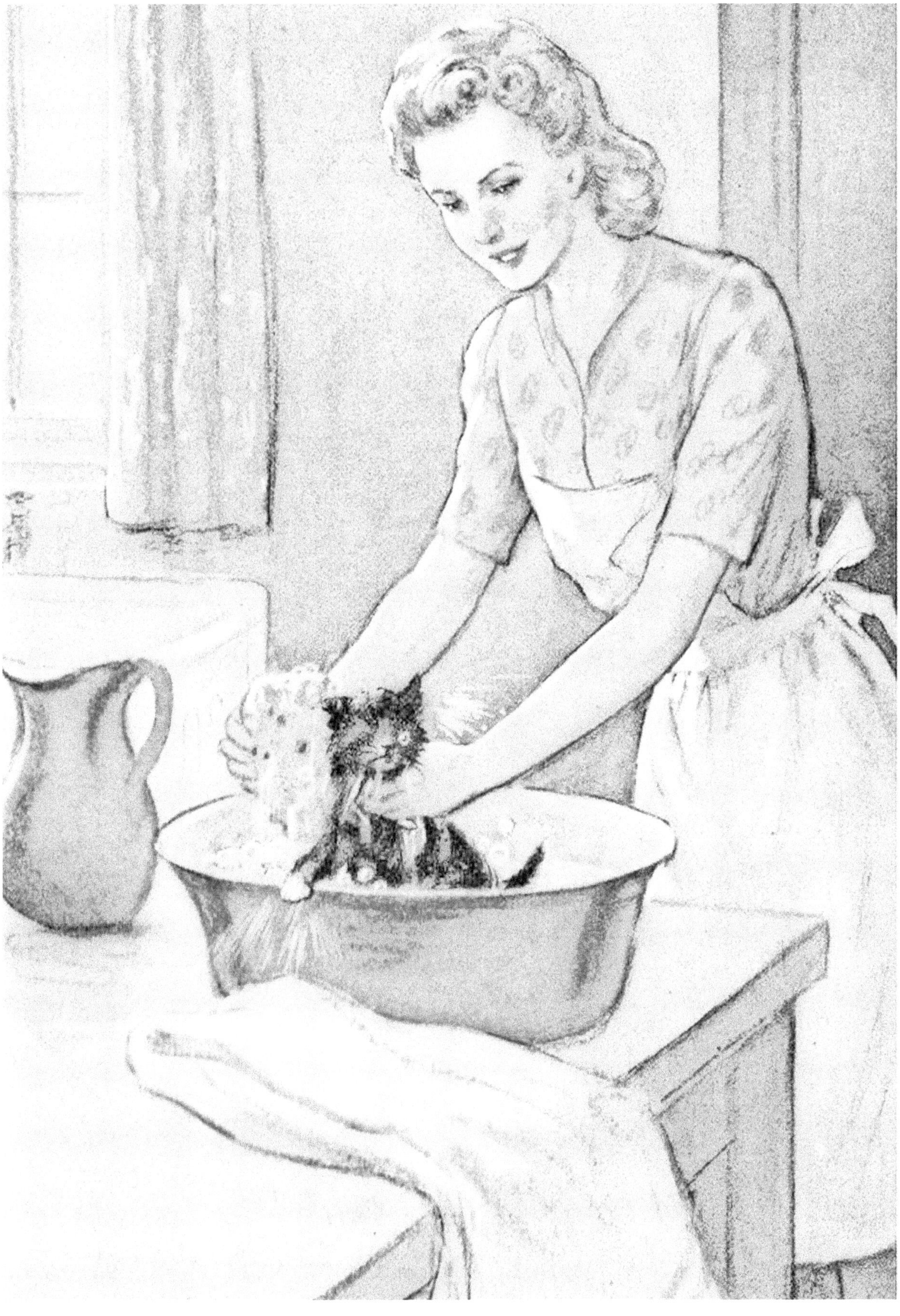

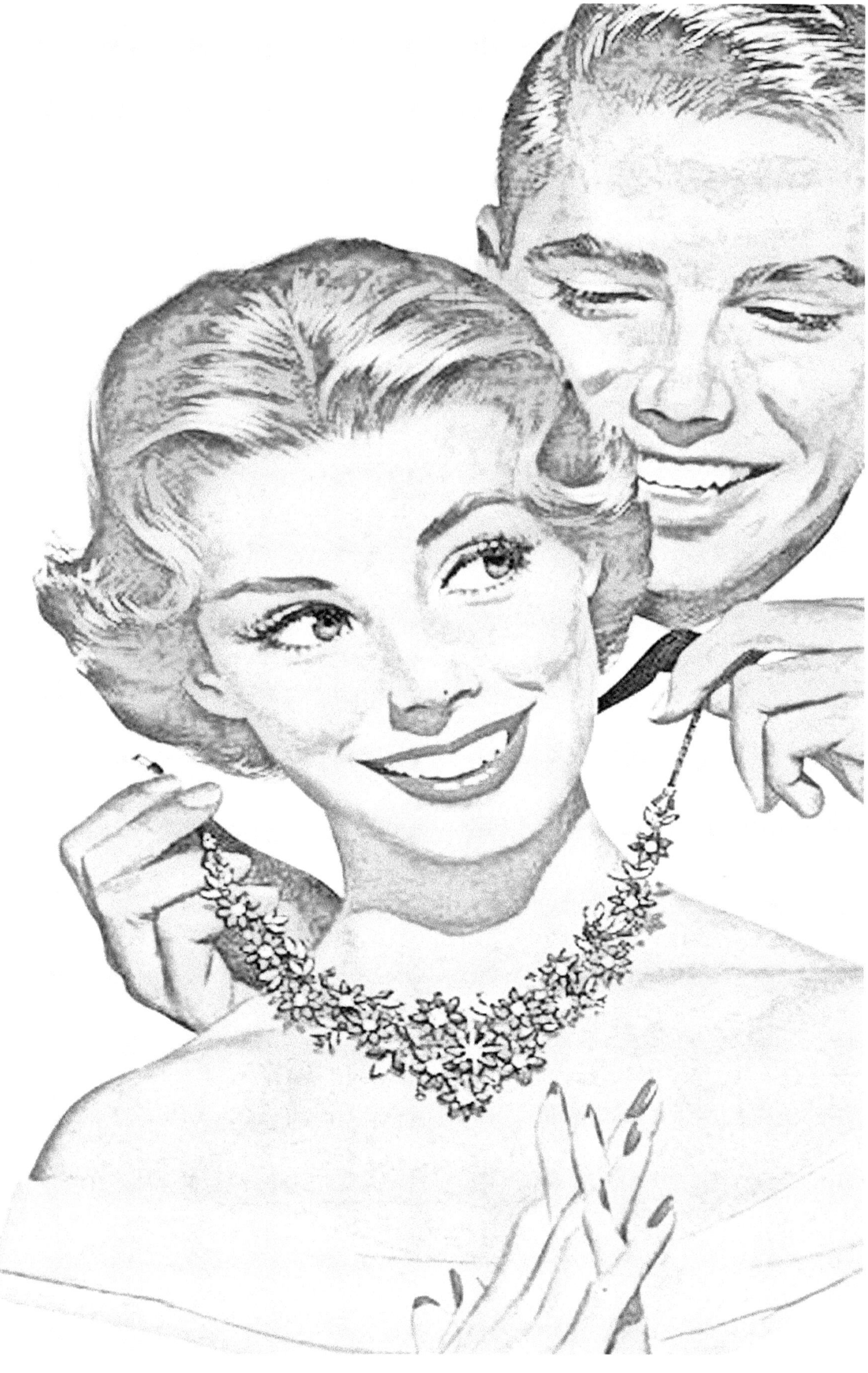

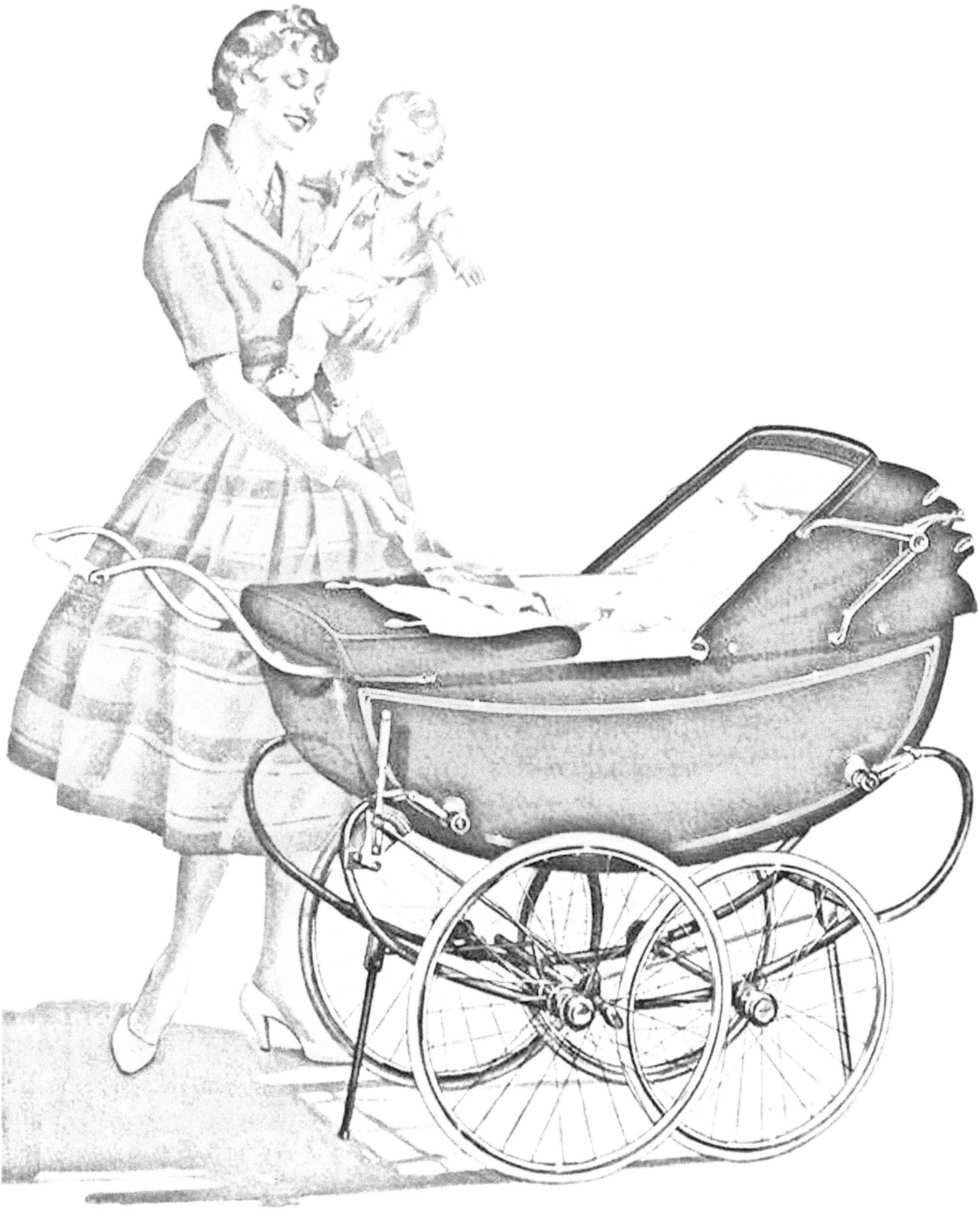

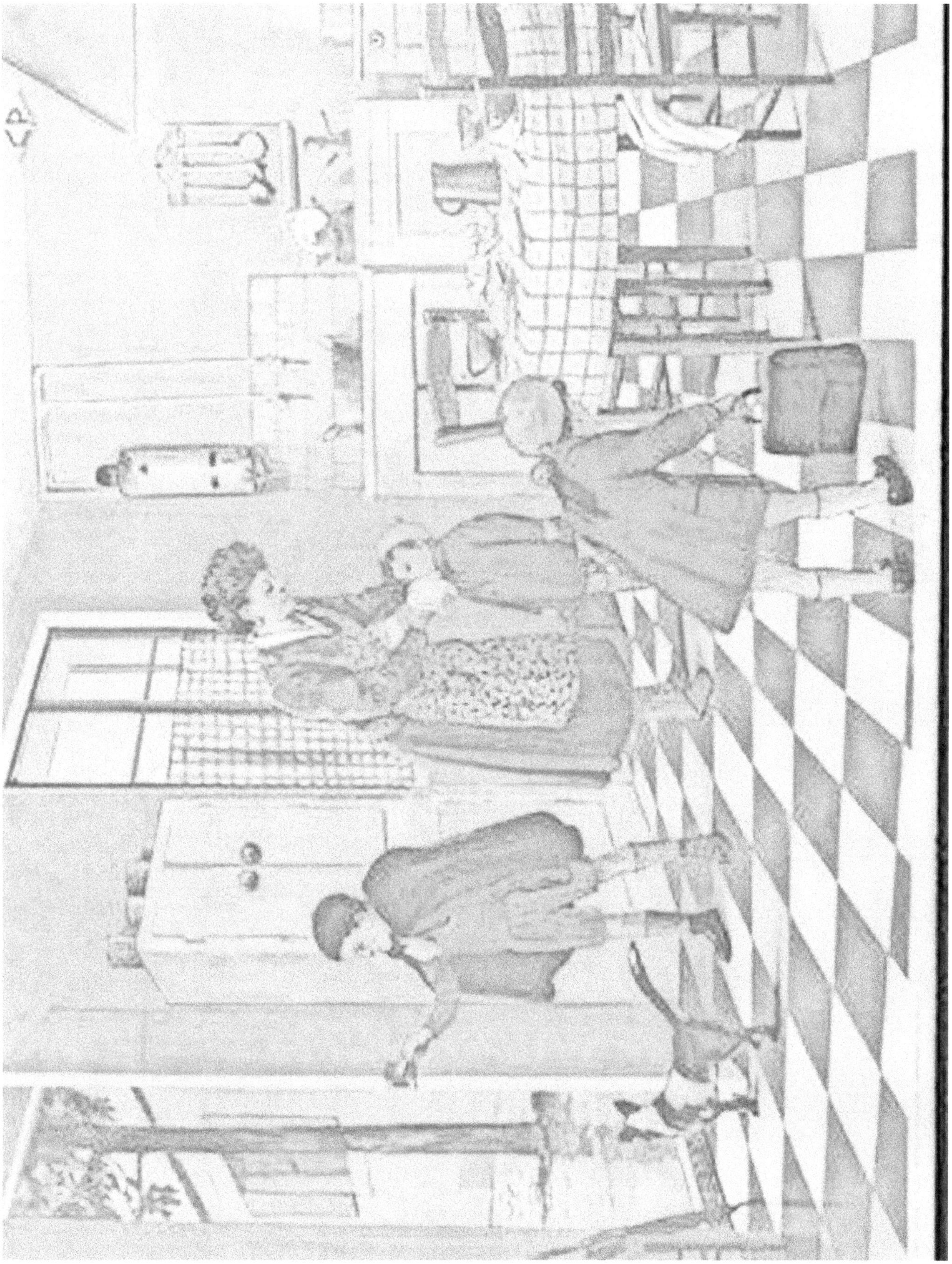

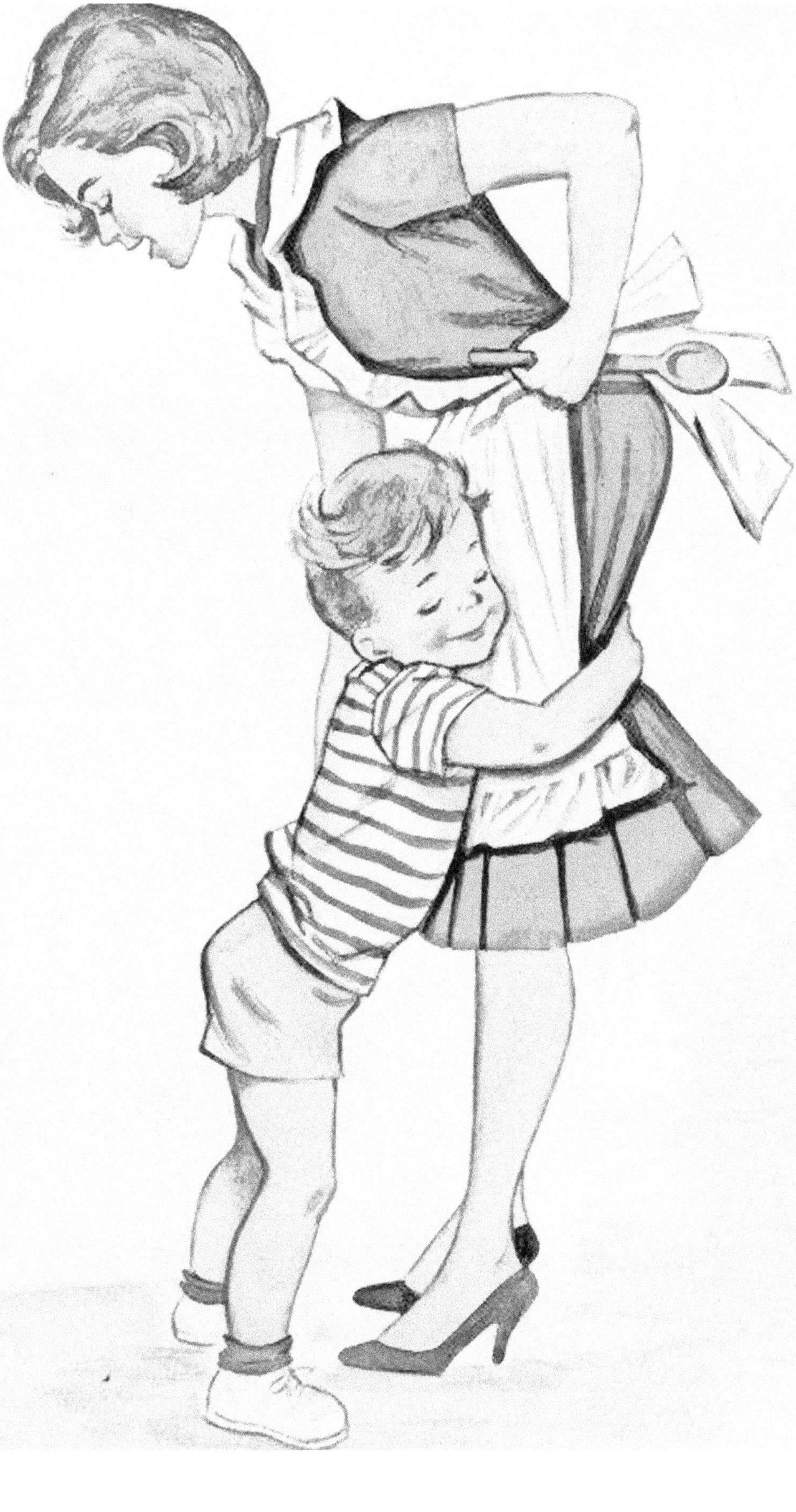

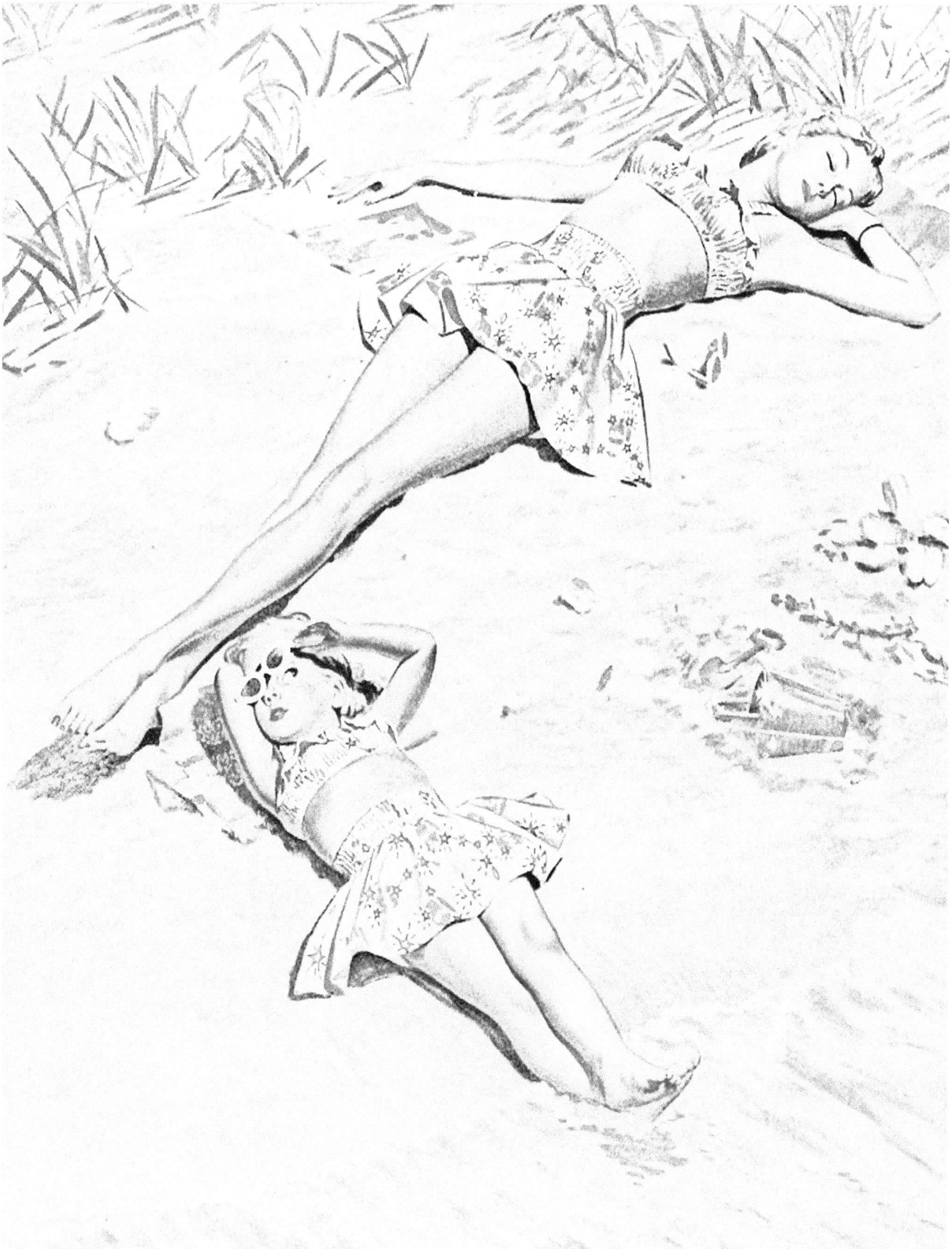

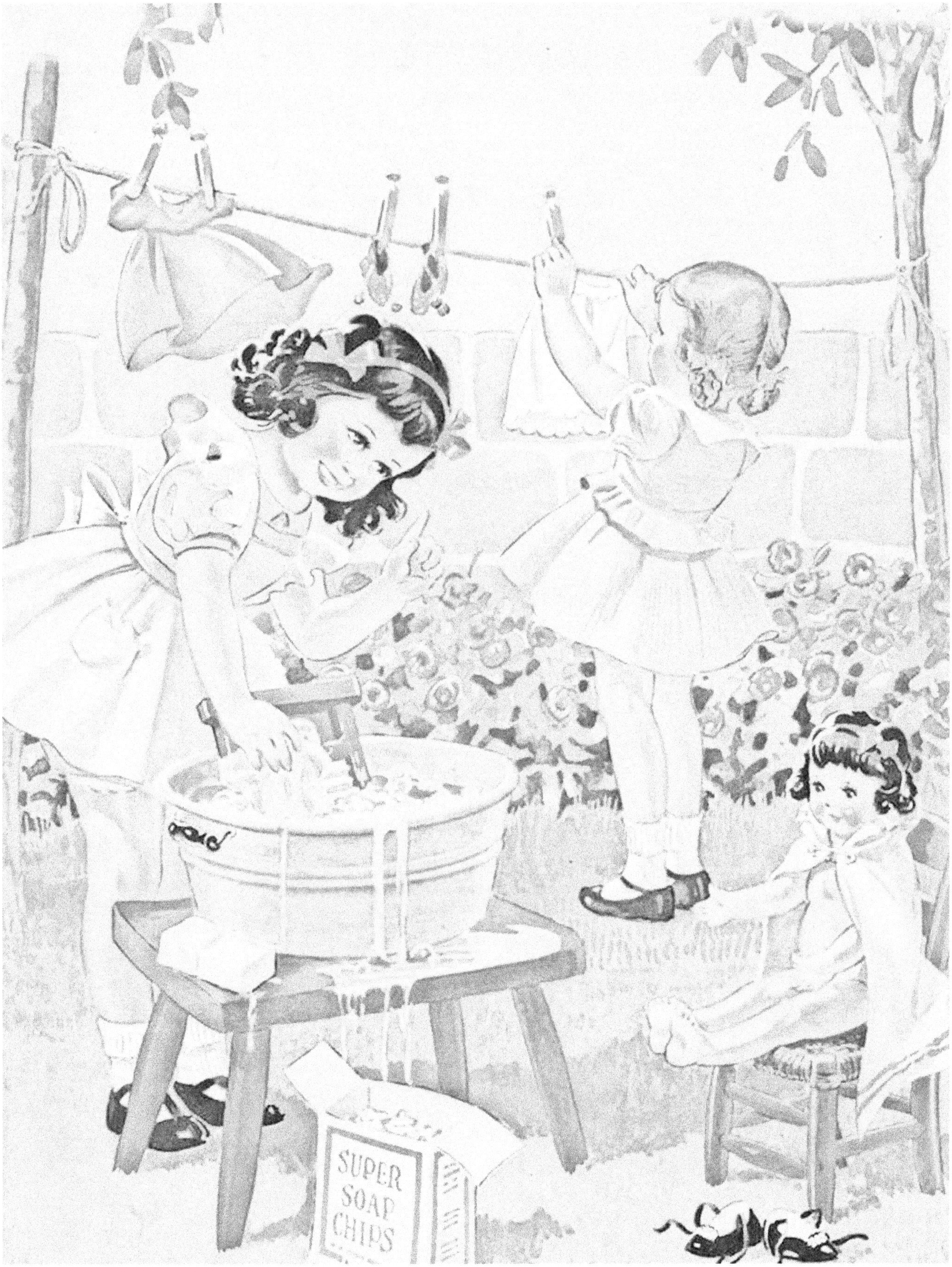
SUPER
SOAP
CHIPS

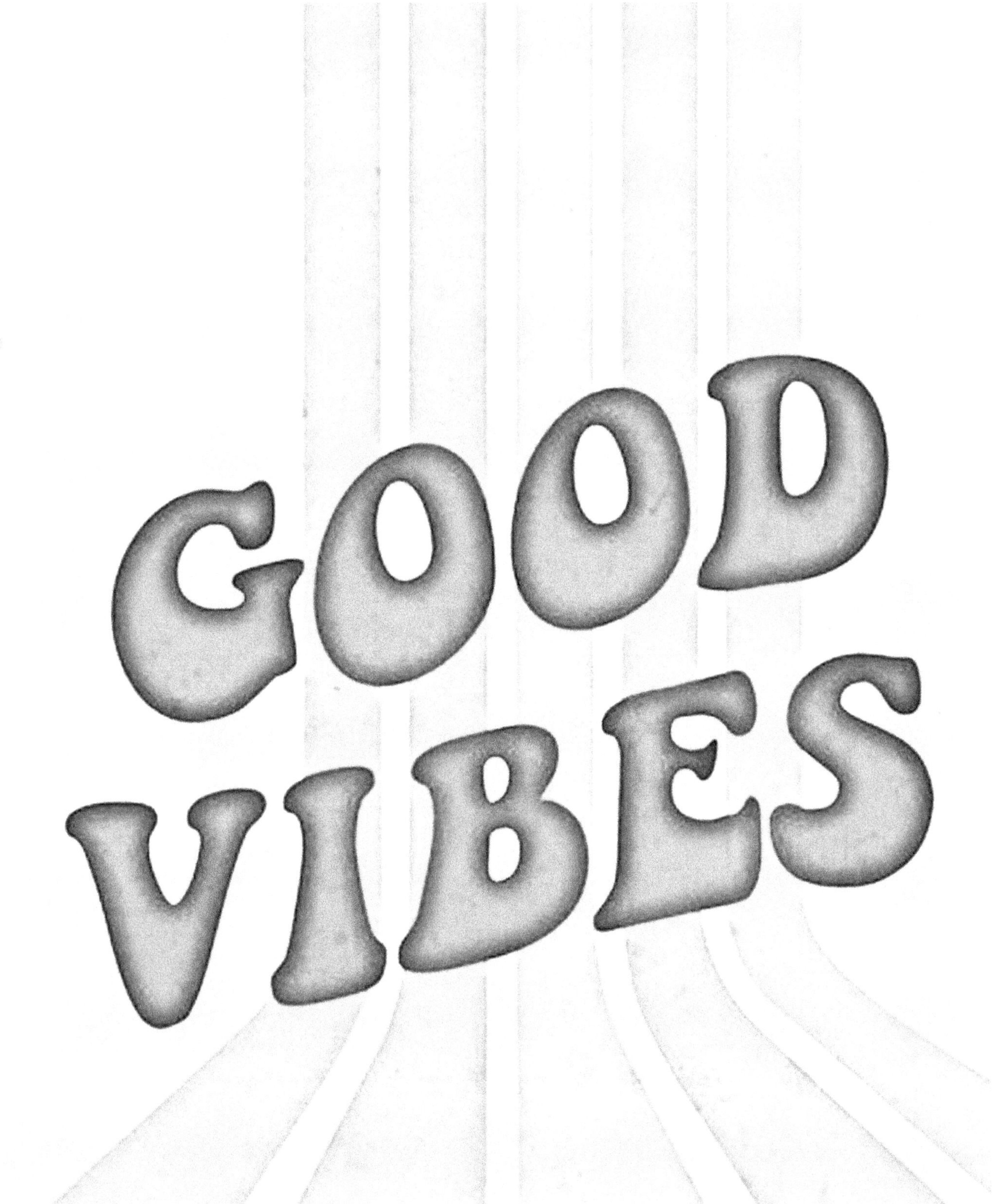
GOOD
VIBES

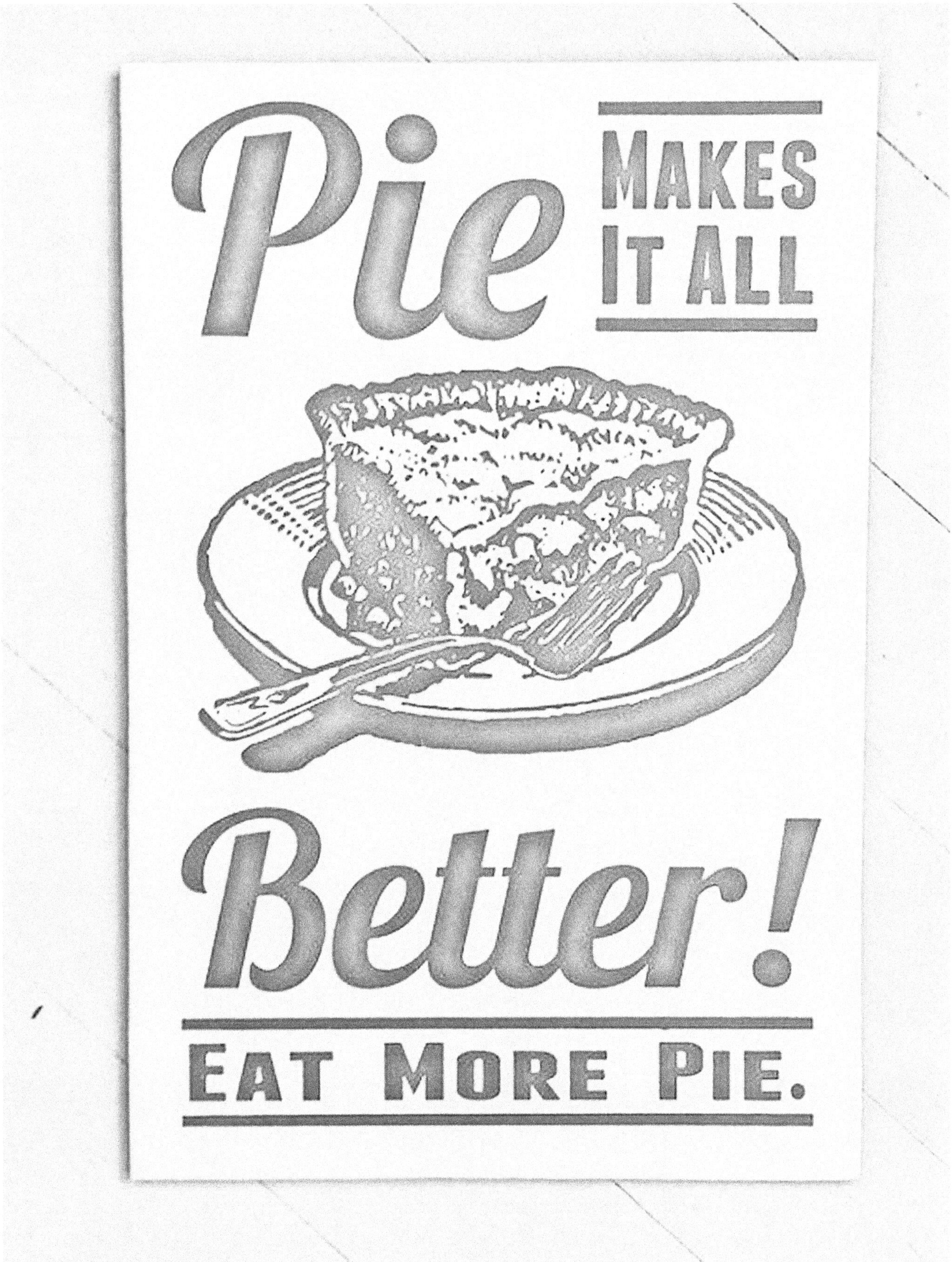
Pie
MAKES IT ALL
Better!
EAT MORE PIE.

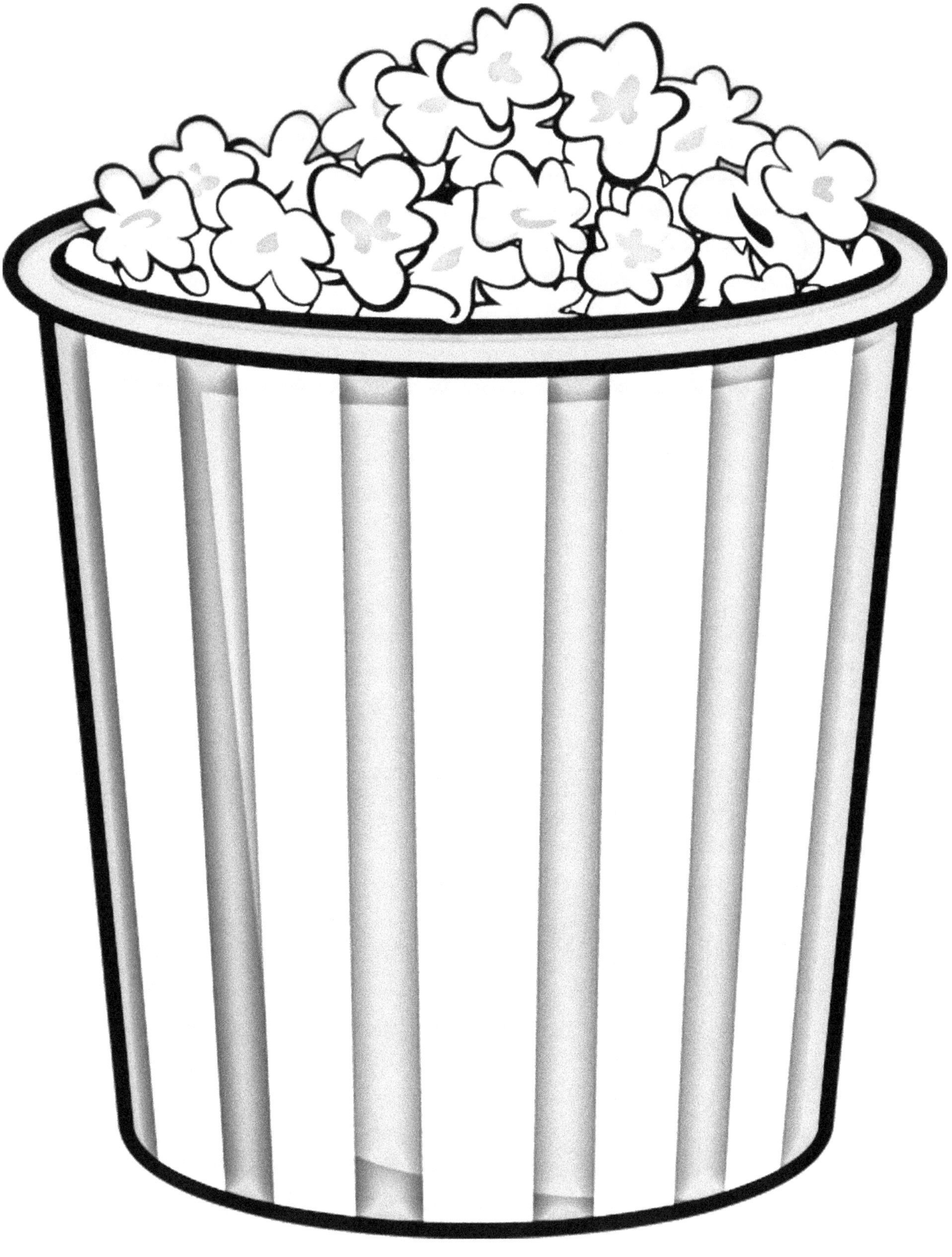

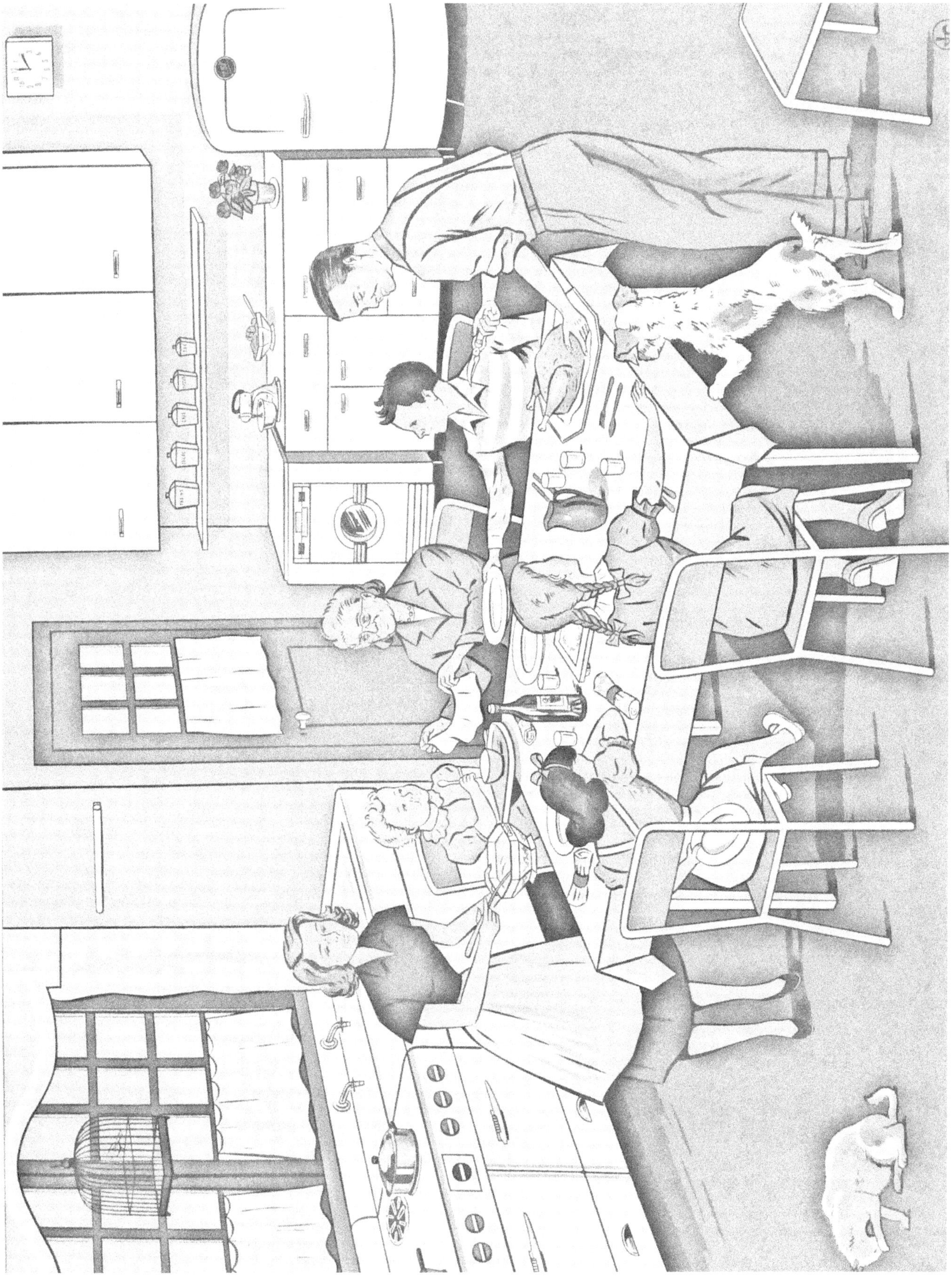

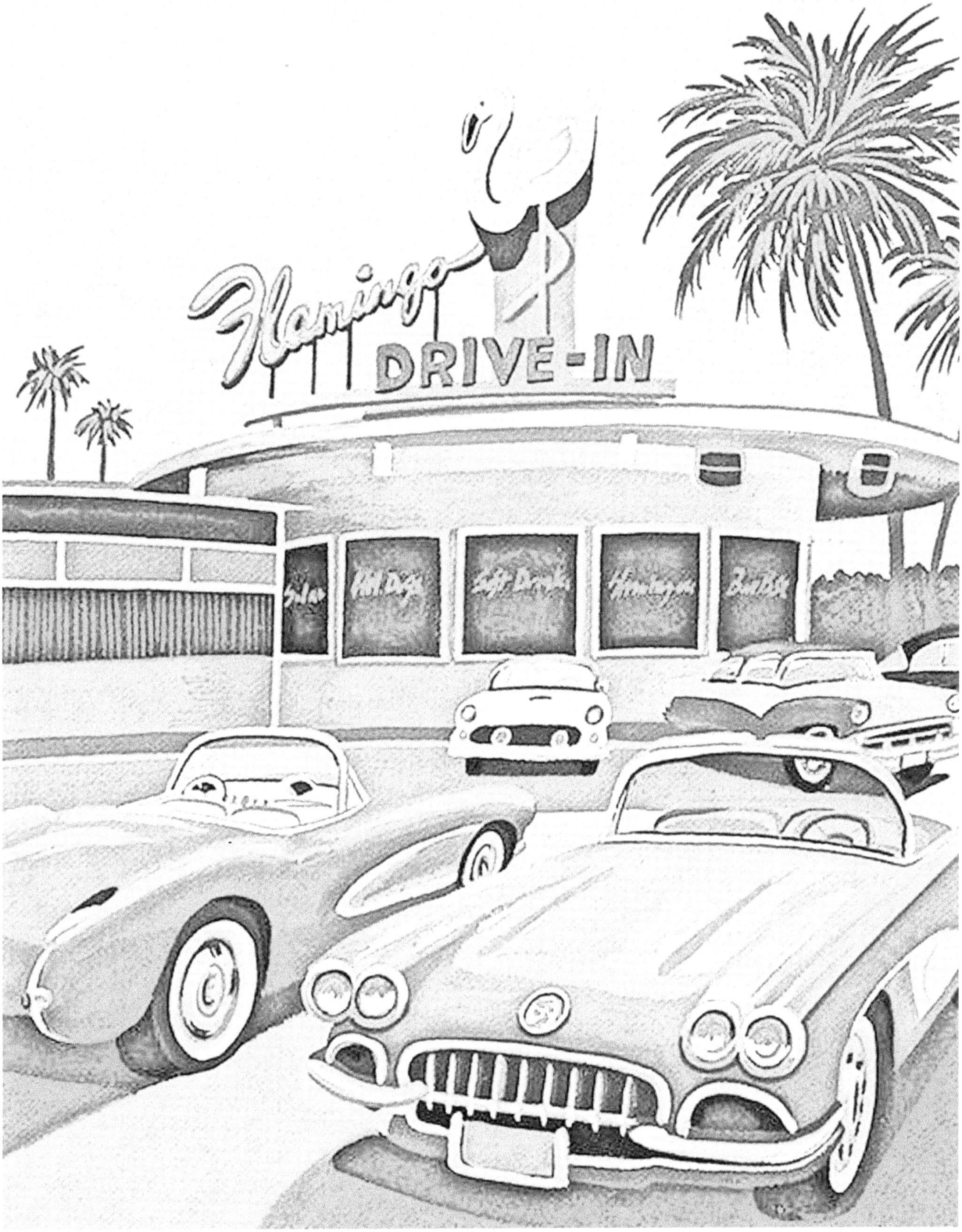
Flamingo
DRIVE-IN

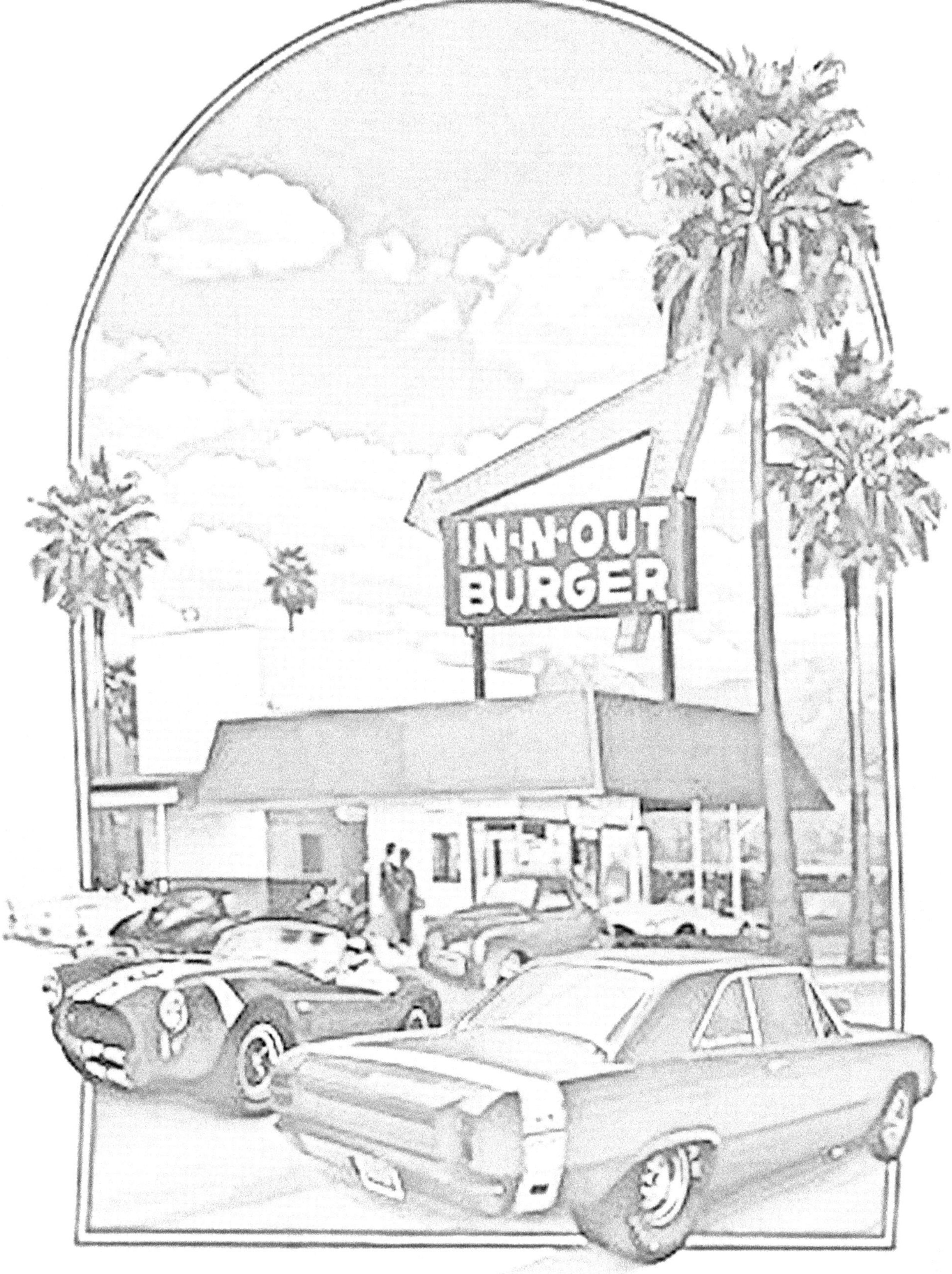
IN-N-OUT
BURGER

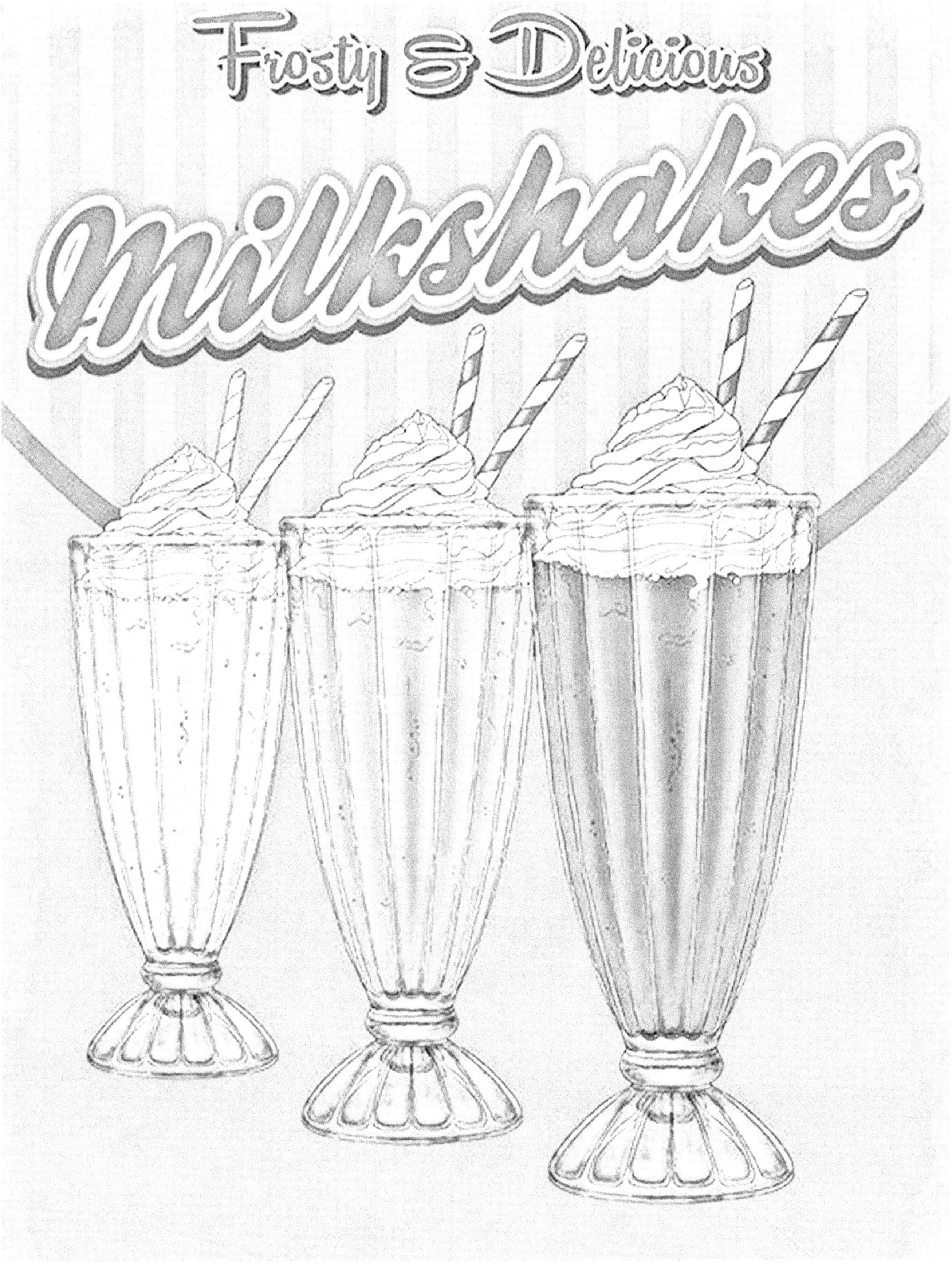
Frosty & Delicious
Milkshakes

DINER

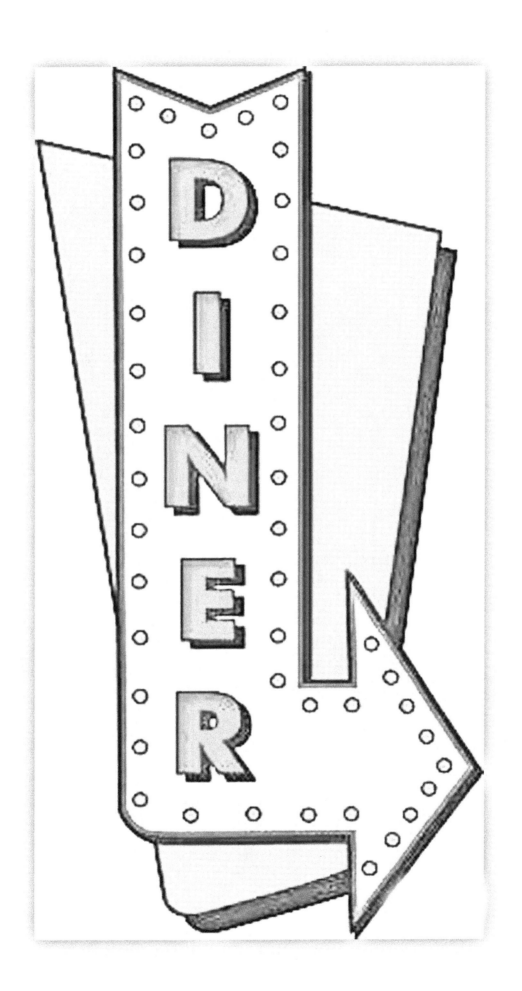

More vintage grayscale coloring books by *Alison Holmes*

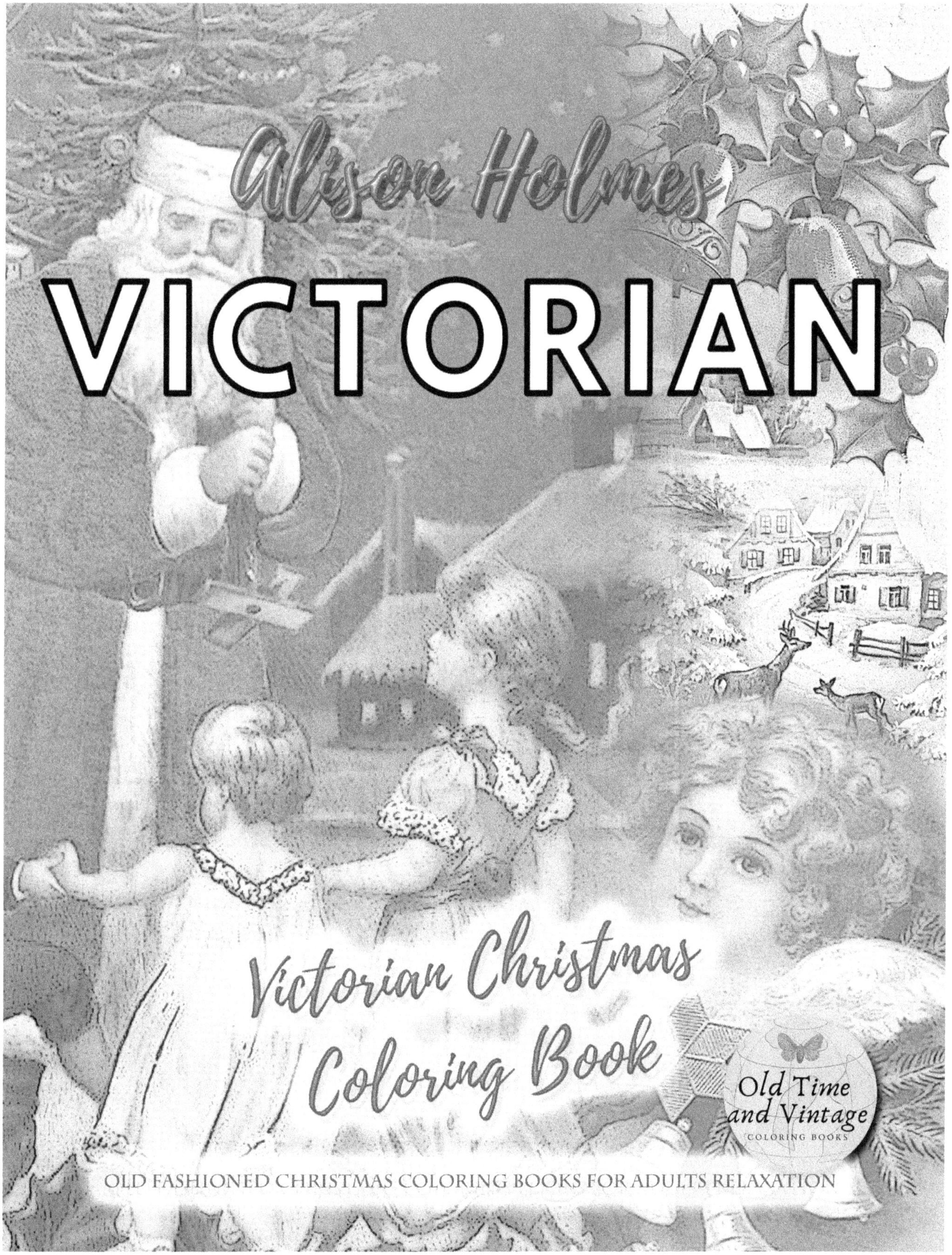
Alison Holmes
VICTORIAN
Victorian Christmas
Coloring Book
Old Time
and Vintage
COLORING BOOKS
OLD FASHIONED CHRISTMAS COLORING BOOKS FOR ADULTS RELAXATION

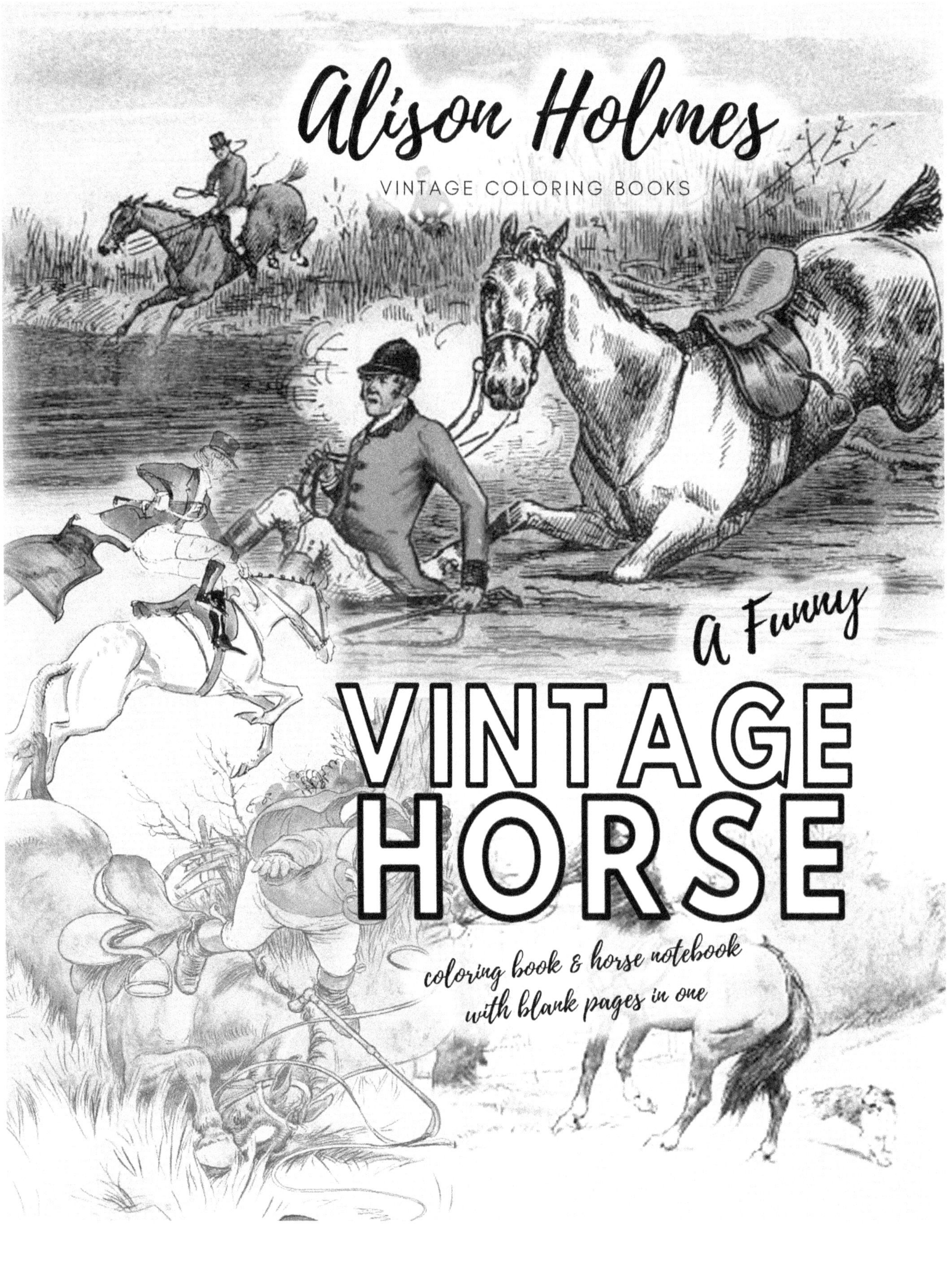

Alison Holmes

VINTAGE COLORING BOOKS

A Funny VINTAGE HORSE

coloring book & horse notebook
with blank pages in one

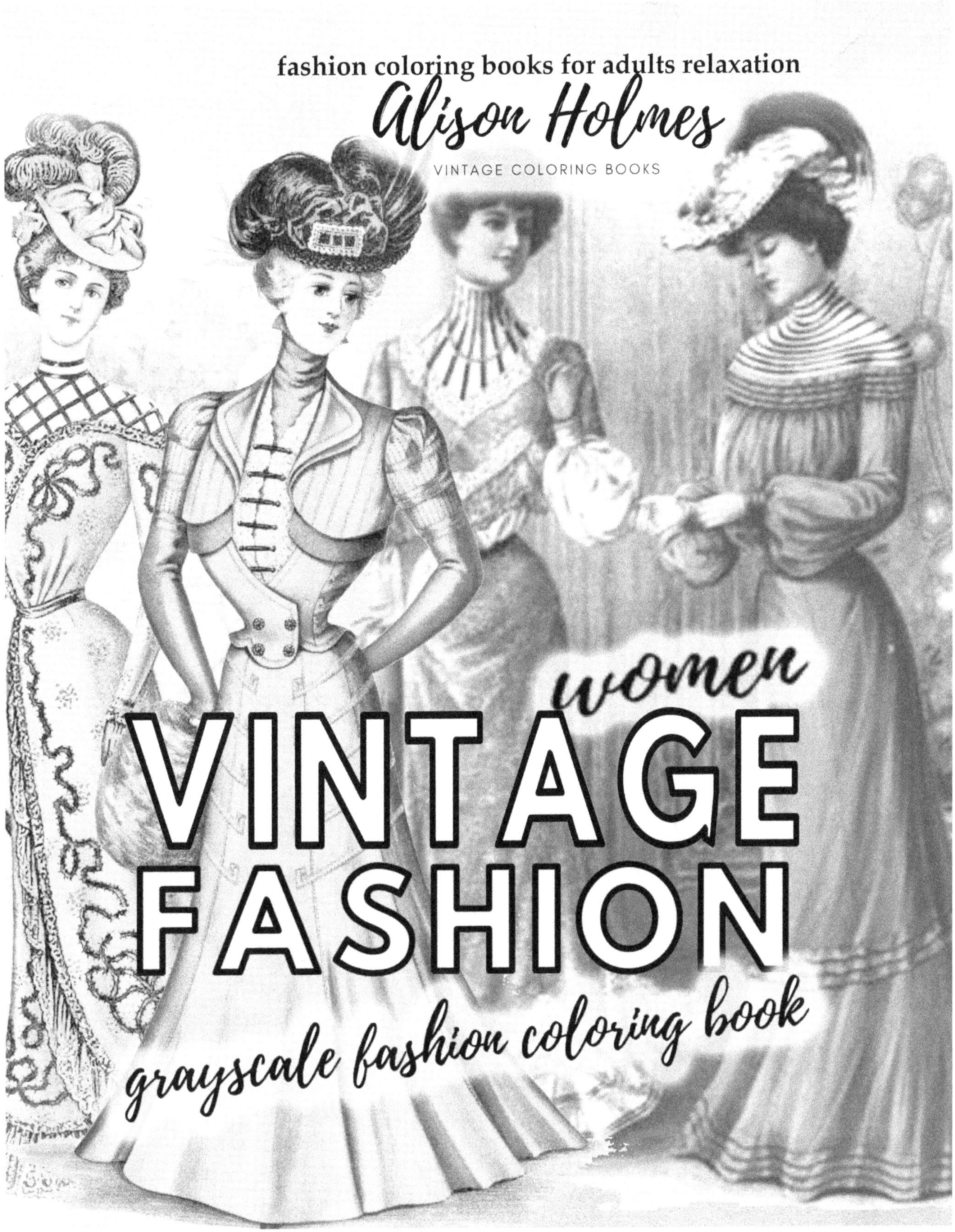
fashion coloring books for adults relaxation
Alison Holmes
VINTAGE COLORING BOOKS
women
VINTAGE
FASHION
grayscale fashion coloring book

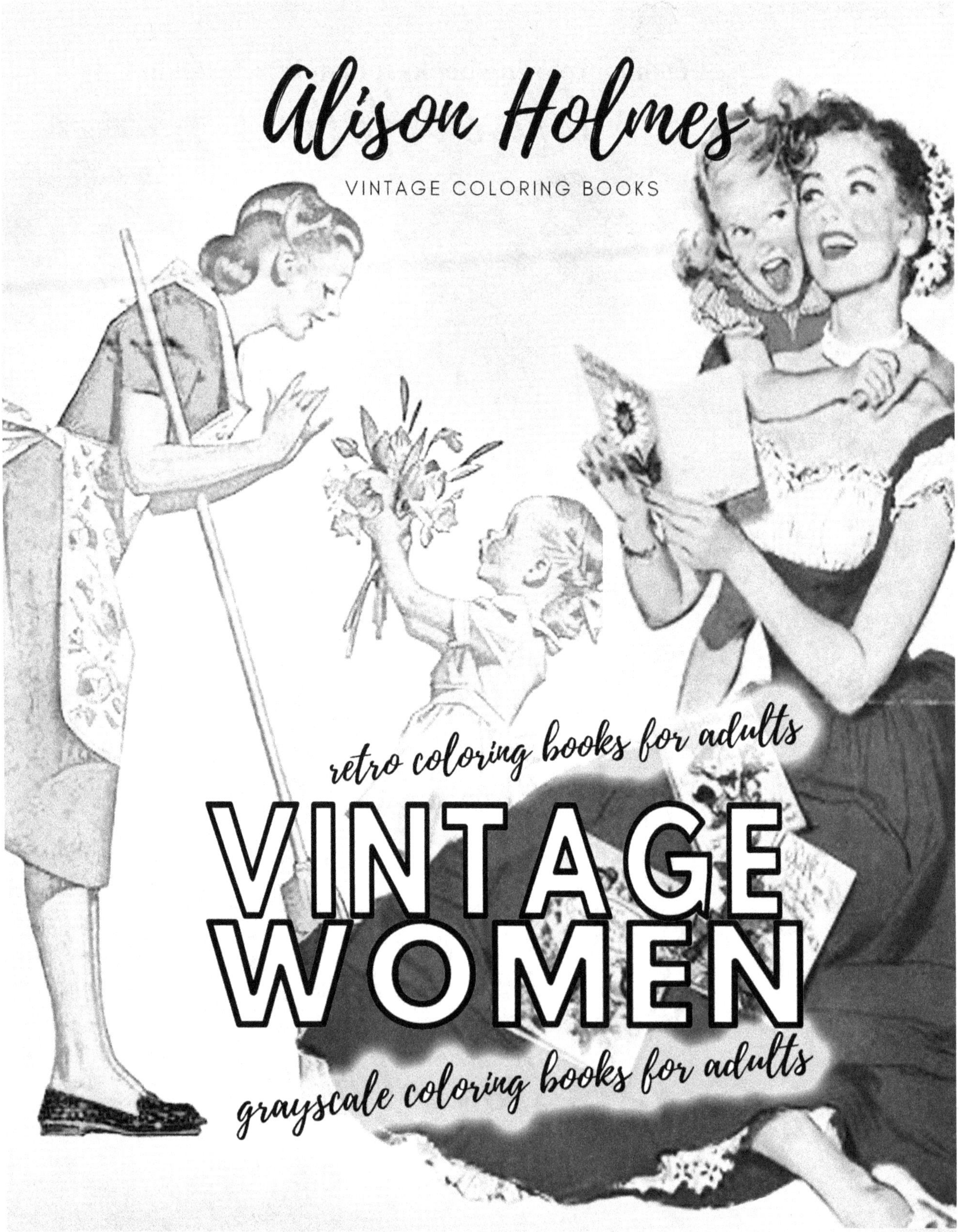
Alison Holmes
VINTAGE COLORING BOOKS
retro coloring books for adults
VINTAGE
WOMEN
grayscale coloring books for adults

CPSIA information can be obtained
at www.ICGtesting.com
Printed in the USA
BVHW020236100323
660165BV00008B/66